NEWSPAPER THEATRE

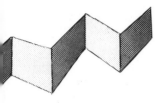

**Creative Play Production
for Low Budgets and No Budgets**

by Alice Morin

**Fearon Teacher Aids
Belmont, California**

Designer: Michelle Taverniti
Illustrator: Joe C. Shines

ISBN 0-8224-6349-0

Printed in the United States of America

1. 9 8 7 6 5 4 3 2

Contents

Introduction

I was 19 and beginning my first summer as a park and recreation supervisor. The major activity on the playgrounds was baseball in some form. If I needed new bats and balls, I only had to stop at the office and request them. After a couple of weeks, though, I discovered baseball was not enough for all of the children or for me. There was no budget for crafts beyond the crayons, coloring books, and colored paper we'd been issued. A drama program? Sure, go ahead, but there's no money for supplies.

Then a discovery. One end of the hall where I took the children for drinks and bathroom was stacked with bundles of old newspapers: the result of a Boy Scout paper drive. I can't credit my own initial creation or recall which children started it, but it wasn't long until the piles of newspapers became a fort, a castle, a sailing ship. As the loosely tied bundles came apart, single sheets were transformed into weapons, treasures, hats, and masks. Thus began what was to become more than thirty years of Newspaper Theatre.

"Please help me. What can I do with all of them?" a desperate teacher at a workshop for creative drama appealed to me. She had 36 students in a drama program. I didn't tell her I had worked with more than

60 in a high school program and a record 86 elementary and middle school students in a summer workshop.

I did tell her that Newspaper Theatre is what to do. Keep some busy with stimulating activity as they make props, costumes, and set pieces. Have others engage in group exercises with newspaper text for scripts. Use sheets with photos for the nonreaders and beginning readers. A small group could look for pictures that look like the characters and scenery and costumes to be used in the play. Cartoon strips can be used this way and also serve as dialogue drills for readers of all ages. Simply instruct the children to read the cartoon dialogue in varying accents or to express feelings. While all of this goes on, you can work with a group on stage. The supervision can be loose while the students experiment with the newspapers. If their efforts need to be reworked, there is no worrisome loss or mess. Wad up the attempt, throw it away, grab another sheet, and try again.

During three decades of teaching and directing drama programs in schools, colleges, recreation programs, adult education, and community theatre, I have rarely had a budget; and when I did, it was a limited one. But newspapers are always available, always useful, always the source of endless discovery. Cut, tear, fold, wad, wet, paste, glue, tape, staple, paint, and mix with other inexpensive materials. When I saw Orson Bean make his famous eucalyptus tree on the Jack Paar show in the early sixties, a whole new aspect of Newspaper Theatre opened before me: newspaper sculpture.

Creative drama with children should be fun. However, hard work, energy drain, and extra stress are predictable in drama programs, especially where production is involved. But, we needn't add to it. We should look for ways to stay as free, fresh, and spontaneous as the eager, young performers who come to us. With Newspaper Theatre we needn't worry about the lack of funds or materials. Our energy can be directed toward guidance and teaching.

I am still using newspapers. The variety of sizes— from comic book ads to tabloid advertising weeklies to the thick, large-sheet dailies—has increased in the past several years. Color, paper, and print have been improved, and newspapers are still available in quantity for no cost. So load the classroom, the recreation room, the workshop, and the backstage area with bundles or stacks of old newspapers, and follow this guide to have fun with Newspaper Theatre.

To acknowledge everyone who worked with me, as Newspaper Theatre evolved over 34 years, would mean a list too long to include here. So, my thanks to all the children who have pretended and played with me over the years. The many parents and teachers also have my gratitude. Three mothers who worked closely with me during the Richmond Community Theatre Summer Workshop are Mary Beth Berger, Marge Helinski, and Luella Golembiewski. Special appreciation to Fred Olds for photos and to my husband, Norm, and my son, Joel, who always help and encourage me.

What Is Newspaper Theatre?

Newspaper Theatre is any use of newspaper to meet the needs of your drama program. Newspaper Theatre is low cost or no cost. It is easy to supply, and it is democratically available to all. It is a source of creative stimulation, limited only by energy and imagination. If you lack storage space for wardrobe, props, and scenery pieces, Newspaper Theatre is the answer. When the production or workshop or exercise is over, throw everything away. Next time, start fresh, start new; new pieces, new creations.

Need hats? Make them from newspaper. If you need a skit or an original play, create a simple story; a simple conflict using the hats for motivation. That's Newspaper Theatre.

Need costumes? Tunics? Armor? Leg or arm wrappings? Capes? Wings? Use newspaper. That's Newspaper Theatre.

Need properties? Swords? Spears? Rifles? Furniture? Logs? Kites? Boxes? Rocks? Use newspaper for built-in safety during stage combat. That's Newspaper Theatre.

Need sets and scenery? Backdrops? Walls? Flowers? Vines? Trees? Texture? Use newspaper: black and white or color; flat surfaces or sculptured.

Need scripts? Take topics, themes, or dialogue from the front page, from interviews, from editorials, the sports page, announcements, and comics. For beginning readers, teachers can read aloud and then lead the discussion and eventual selection of characters, plot, and conflict. A dramatic story about firefighting or lifesaving or extreme weather conditions can quickly be adapted to improvisation, and eventually a script can be written by a teacher or the older students. This approach to a script can be particularly effective with news items that have strong impact, such as a local storm, a robbery, or a national sports event. There are scripts galore in a pile of newspaper. That's Newspaper Theatre.

Need motivation? Use newspapers. Read to the youngest; let the older readers read in groups or with your guidance. Reenact a report of heroism, a battle, a ceremony, a natural tragedy, the final inning of an important baseball game. From these simple exercises, a director and the students can find avenues for stimulation, motivation for a new direction. That's Newspaper Theatre.

Need exercises? Use newspaper articles for diction, dialogue to practice accents, vocabulary building, and subjects for characterizations. Most newspaper text can be easily read by average and above-average readers in the upper elementary grades. Beginning readers can use comics, large-print advertisements—such as those for food and clothing, and the special publications supplied to elementary classrooms. Don't forget foreign language newspapers for bilingual students. That's Newspaper Theatre.

Need audition material? Read from newspapers. Teachers can read to beginning readers for visualization or have them repeat words and phrases to hear their voice quality and strength. Older readers with advanced reading skills can read directly from newspapers. That's Newspaper Theatre.

Newspaper Theatre is fun at your fingertips. Newspaper Theatre will unfold for you as you follow the simple instructions in the coming chapters. Use these guides as they apply to your needs. Enjoy the luxury of a material that is still plentiful and free and that has endless possible applications to your drama programs.

▶ **Safety First.** Never in all my years with Newspaper Theatre have I had a fire, because the message is always clearly sent out: *Newspaper Theatre and open flame do not mesh.* Flammable material must be used sensibly. The best way to avoid problems with flammable material is to use it and do away with it. Don't keep it around; Newspaper Theatre is more process than product. When you keep pieces overnight or through a production, store them wisely.

▶ **Soap and Water.** Washing the hands is usually necessary after any Newspaper Theatre activity. Some newspaper inks rub off easily. But many now have the more expensive low-rub inks. So if you are very fastidious, select your newspaper accordingly. For Newspaper Theatre, children should be dressed in suitable, washable play clothes, as is advisable for any theatre or craft-making project.

▶ **Attachments.** Newspaper can be held together in many ways. Use glue, paste (flour and water is cheap in quantity), staples, straight pins, clothes pins, bobby pins, paper clips, tacks, wire ties, string, or tape (transparent, masking, duct, or electrical). Whatever does the job at the time is the best choice. Never use fasteners with sharp ends, such as pins, tacks, or staples, on costumes or properties that children will handle. These fasteners should be used only temporarily until glue or paste or ties are applied, or on scenery that is out of reach. All use of sharp fasteners must be closely supervised by teachers.

2

Making Hats from Newspaper

Begin with hats. Draw from a classic: Christopher Robin's soldier hat can be found in illustrations of A. A. Milne's *Winnie the Pooh* stories and poems.

The two most familiar examples of practical newspaper sculpture are the newspaper envelope hats worn by workmen to protect their hair from grease and soot, and the newspaper cone for carrying fried potatoes or chips from the fish-and-chips vendor. Both of these examples are from nineteenth-century England, and both can still be found in use today.

You might talk about some history, economics, and sociology as you fold. The most frequent illustrations and references to practical newspaper sculpture come out of nineteenth-century England because that's where the Industrial Revolution started. Once technology provided enough newspapers for most people to have access to them, creative consumers found many new ways to use them. It wasn't long until newspapers were available to all city children and to most rural boys and girls. The hat-making and kite-making that preceded the glut of toys available to today's children were an important part of play.

Good research projects in the classroom can grow from the pursuit of pictures showing newspapers recycled as hats and kites.

THE BASIC HAT

The basic, envelope-style hat begins with three to six sheets of newspaper and adds two folds to the original vertical fold. Hat size is determined by the size of the newspaper—tabloid, ad sheets, or large sheets—and by the size of the openings left after folding.

▼ The Basic Hat

1. Lay the newspaper sheets on a table or floor with the vertical fold at the top. Three to six sheets is a good thickness.

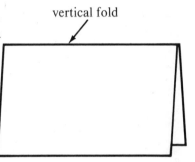

vertical fold

2. Fold the top corners toward the center.

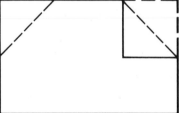

3. Make the crown flatter by folding less of the corners. Make it more pointed by bringing the sides together.

4. Putting your hands inside the hat, fold up about 4 inches of the top layer. Turn over and repeat.

The basic hat can be used for soldiers, sailors, jesters, or Robin Hood and his merry men. Put on the hats, look at each other, and ask who you are. You are Napoleon. You work at a fast-food drive-in. Answers lead to ideas for sketches and scenes.

BIRD AND ANIMAL MASKS

Change the fold, cut eyeholes, attach pieces, and you have **bird and animal heads and masks**. Use sheets that are large enough to drop down over the head. Bird and animal heads can be painted or colored for a more realistic look.

▼ Bird or Animal Head

1. Fold one end diagonally for a beak.

2. Fold the other end vertically to close the back of the head or mask.

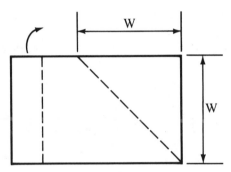

3. Cut eyeholes to size.

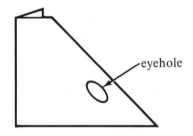

eyehole

Ears

Glue, paste, or tape ears cut from two or three thicknesses of paper.

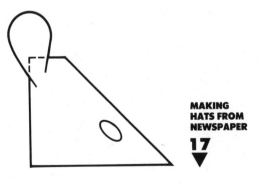

Noses

1. For the basic nose, roll two thicknesses of paper to make a tube. Use a long roll for a trunk and a shorter one for a snout. Taper one end as you roll.

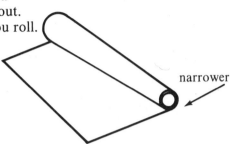

narrower

2. Glue, paste, or tape tube inside beak end of head.
Bend a long tube for a trunk.

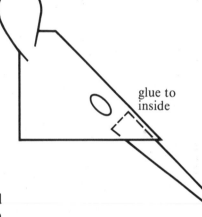

glue to inside

3. Glue, paste, or tape a short tube for a snout. Add a paper circle on the end to make a different snout.

CONICAL HAT

The taller a conical hat, the greater the number of sheets of newspaper that are needed. Three or four sheets is a good beginning to test stiffness and body. Experiment to see what is workable.

▼ Conical Hat

1. This shape is cut from a newspaper sheet opened flat.

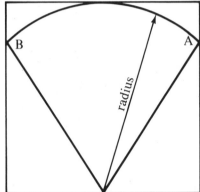

2. Bring corner A to meet corner B and secure with tape or glue after you shape the cone and place it on the child's head to determine head size. To keep cone smooth, fasten edges while holding hat point downward.

Cone-shaped hats can be used to stimulate creative play or build a sketch. The cone-shaped hat becomes a dunce cap, a witch's hat, a wizard's hat, a space creature, and more. And don't forget Maid Marion's conical hat, with a paper scarf floating from the point—the complement to the Robin Hood basic-shaped hat. The hats you build from cones are potential patterns for more permanent hats from other materials.

PERIOD HATS

Taping, gluing, or pasting folds can **increase the life of a hat** and also make it more manageable for the younger student. Permanent pieces should be painted, lacquered, and secured. Materials for decorating and strengthening newspaper products will be discussed in Chapter 7. Hats for one session, or for use in exercises, should be quickly made and discarded or sent home after the session.

With paint and additional pieces, you can create sophisticated, reusable period hats. These hats are often expensive to rent, but the newspaper hat, built with care and treated to last, can be a valuable supplement to a wardrobe. Examples of these are Prussian helmets, Foreign Legion hats, bishops' miters, crowns, pillbox hats, and any other hat you need. Begin with good illustrations from costume books, make the basic shape, and go from there.

Many period hats begin with a **narrow hat** (a variation of the basic hat) or with a **basic crown**. To make a narrower hat, add another set of folds to the basic hat.

▼ Narrow Hat

1. Begin with the basic hat. Fold each side in toward the center.

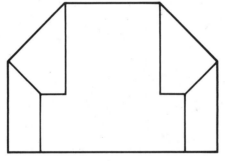

fold   fold

2. These folds will have to be secured with paste, glue, or tape.

▼ Prussian Helmet

1. Fold as for Narrow Hat. Fold each side toward the center. Try on; adjust for size. Glue or tape down folded edges.

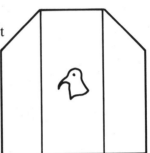

fold

2. Accent with paper or painted designs to suggest metalwork.

▼ Bishop's Miter

Make a narrow hat. Add a pointed half ellipse to the front and decorate with painted or cut paper designs

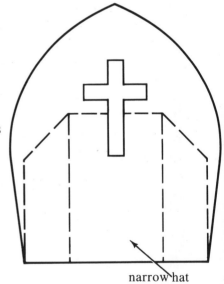

narrow hat

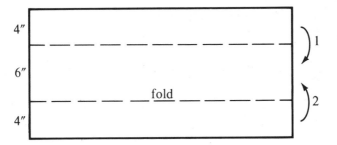

▼ Basic Crown

1. Fold a 14-inch-wide rectangle in thirds, as shown in the illustration above.

2. Adjust folded strip to fit child's head. Attach ends with tape or glue.

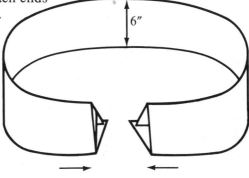

▼ Royal Crown

Glue, tape, or paste points cut from three or four thicknesses of newspaper to basic crown.

▼ Foreign Legion Hat

1. Begin with basic crown. Cut bill as shown above from one thickness of newspaper.

2. Glue, tape, or paste bill to basic crown.

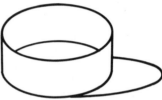

3. Cut small rectangle from one thickness of newspaper for the cloth that hangs from the back of the hat. Attach rectangle with glue, paste, or tape to back of basic crown.

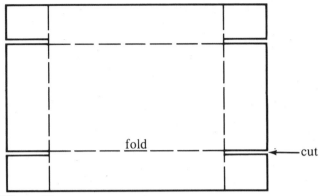

▼ Pillbox Hat

1. Begin with three or four flat sheets of newspaper. Cut and fold as shown above.

2. Fold at corners as shown. Place on child's head to adjust to head size. Glue, paste, or tape at corners.

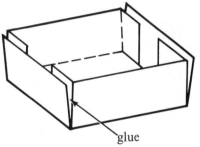

glue

3. Add feather cut from a single sheet of newspaper. Attach feather to hat with glue, tape, or paste. The shaft of the feather is made from a tube of newspaper rolled as tightly as possible.

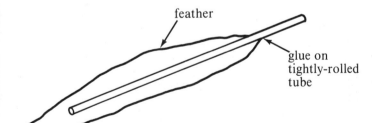

feather

glue on tightly-rolled tube

4. For the veil, fold a single sheet of newspaper in quarters, and cut a lacy pattern as shown.

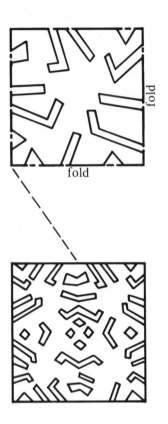

5. Unfold veil and attach to front of pillbox hat with glue, paste, or tape.

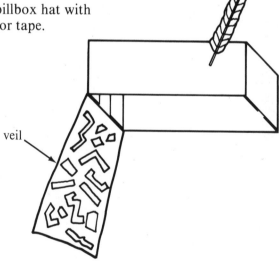

veil

WIGS

Fright wigs, clown wigs, or fantasy character wigs can be created by cutting an oval or circle to fit the top of the head and attaching curls, starting at the edge, with tape or glue. Further directions for curls can be found in Chapter 5.

▼ Curls

1. Roll a single sheet into a 1- to 2-inch diameter roll. Dampen roll. Cut into 1- to 2-inch lengths, and let dry before unrolling.

2. Attach curls by starting at outside of oval.

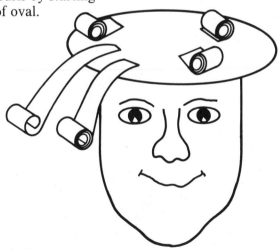

Newspaper Theatre from newspaper hats can fill a unit, a semester, or lengthy workshop sessions. It is essential to master the material but not to allow the construction to dominate. The goals should be clear. Newspaper provides quick, free, easy-to-make stimulants for make-believe, pretending and imagining, and creating. Time-consuming, permanent hat building belongs in the stagecraft and technical-skill-building parts of a drama program. Don't mix your purposes. Which is first: the hat or the need for a hat?

3

Making Costumes from Newspaper

Costumes from newspapers, even the most quickly put together, can provide impressive visual displays for assembly and classroom programs where limited time and money curtail costume construction. Newspaper tunics can bring design and visual interest to what would otherwise be a disparate, even scraggly, group.

As you did with hats, decide how much durability and detail are necessary for costumes. If durability is necessary, extra care must be taken in building the pieces. To the very young, who are more free and imaginative, the simplest pieces will be acceptable. Older children will need more detail and appearance of reality in their costumes. For the students who are absorbed with the craft, costumes may be completed at home to allow the group session to be used for creative drama purposes.

DRESSES AND TUNICS

Begin with a **simple dress or tunic**—call it whatever you wish. Take a single sheet, cut a hole at the fold to size, and drop it over the head. With uniform tunics you can differentiate armies, nations, families, or groups. Use newspaper sheets with colored ink or plain black and white. Use glossy pages from Sunday magazines. Paste, glue, or tape on trim. (See page 57 for trim ideas.)

▼ Dress or Tunic

Use a large sheet of newspaper. Cut an opening at the fold large enough to fit over the head.

cut

Newspaper tunics and dresses are usually not re-usable, but duplicates are quickly and easily made for dress rehearsals or even for replacement during performances. Reinforce at the shoulder ends and neckhole with tape or another sheet of glued or pasted paper to make the piece more durable if the part requires much movement or if the piece must be removed and put back on during the play. Cut to give a better fit to smaller children. To add length, connect another sheet at the bottom with a fold and tape or glue.

CAPES

Capes are quick and lend themselves to costumes for royalty, space creatures, or the perennially popular super-heroes and super-heroines. What nursery school or elementary school wardrobe ever has enough capes for all the aspiring Batmen, Robins, Catwomen, or Spidermen? Reach for the newspapers and there's a cape for everyone in minutes.

▼ Capes

1. Make the fold toward one end of a large sheet, and cut neckhole as for a tunic.

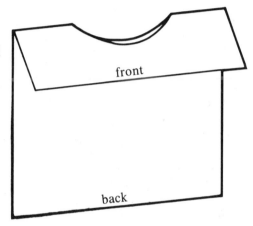

2. A more manageable cape can be made from a single sheet of newspaper and a piece of ribbon or string taped or glued at each of the top corners. Tie loosely around the neck.

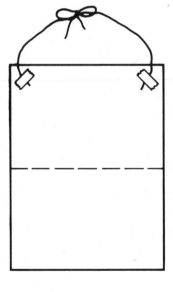

ARM AND LEG COVERINGS

For gauntlets or leg armor or for boots for spacepeople
or pirates, use single sheets of newspaper, or use several
layers for stiffness and durability. For a performance or
use beyond a few minutes, wrap tape at wrist and elbow
or at ankle and knee. Or use ribbons or colored string,
which add decoration, too. The leg and arm wrappings
adhere best to long sleeves and pant legs, but clothing
should be washable.

▼ Arm and Leg Coverings

Place sheet against arm or
leg and mark length with
pencil or crayon. Cut and
tape or glue together.

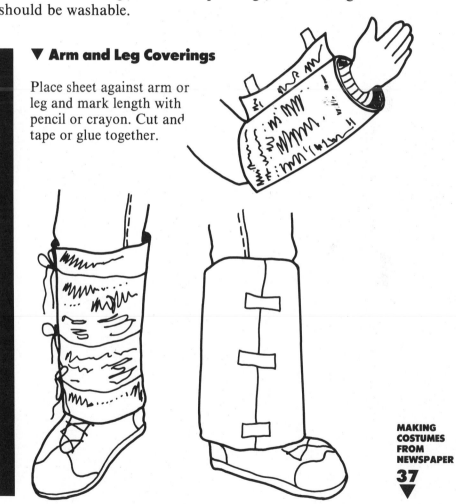

ACCESSORIES AND DECORATION

Paper sculpture can be used to add texture and detail to costumes. Building up layers, rolling, and folding for wristbands, ankle bands, shoulder epaulets, ammunition belts, and jewelry can help make pieces more permanent to supplement wardrobes. Layering strengthens a cape, tunic, or belt and makes it less likely to tear. **Paper fans and paper chains** attached to shoulders, sleeves, or legs give added depth and texture.

▼ Chain

Interlock paper strips made into circles with glue, tape, or paste. Vary the chain by changing the width or length of the strips.

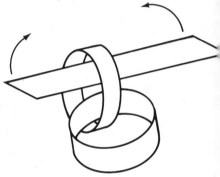

▼ Fan

Paper fans of any size can be quickly folded and attached with tape or glue.

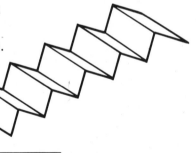

alternate folds

Jewelry is created by hanging chains around the neck or wrists. Pendants can be cut from paper and glued to the chain for royalty. A "jewel" can be cut from paper and glued to a chain link.

Epaulets are ovals or rectangles cut from newspaper and glued to the shoulder of the tunic.

Ammo belts can go around the waist or across the chest (which means you don't have to cut it to fit waist size). Paper rolls can serve as bullets.

▼ Ammunition Belt

1. Cut the belt from several thicknesses of newspaper. Adjust size and tape or staple together.

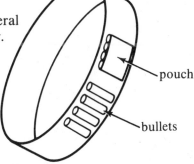

pouch

bullets

2. For the pouch, glue four rolled paper "bullets" together and cover with a rectangle of paper slightly larger than the group of bullets. Glue or paste pouch onto belt. Glue or paste additional "bullets" onto belt.

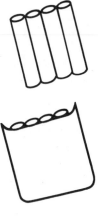

4

Making Properties from Newspaper

Using newspaper for replaceable props is apparently practiced around the world. A recent performance by professional acrobats from Taiwan required a paper hoop for the agile actors to dive through. Newspaper was used to cover the hoop. I was too far away to tell, but it would have been interesting to know if the newspaper was printed with Chinese characters and carried from home, or drawn from a more accessible pile backstage or in a greenroom and printed in Detroit.

A property becomes the real thing in the eye and imagination of the beholder. Invariably, if the student performer believes the object is what he or she wishes it to be, the other performers and the audience will believe as well. The younger the performer, the easier the suspension of disbelief. Convincing others to accept a simple newspaper property as the real object it represents can be a good exercise for stimulating make-believe and play.

Devise exercises in concentration around simple newspaper props. The tube from a roll of newspaper is a telescope. Make us believe it, Galileo. Let the snowball melt in your hand. It looks like a wad of newspaper, but can you feel the cold? A pile of boulders rolling down a mountainside over struggling mountain climbers is a marvelously freeing exercise in acting and movement for

41
▼

all ages. Snowball fights with a rapidly made pile of small newspaper wads will break the ice with a new, too-frosty group.

FURNITURE

The best properties, especially for youngsters, are ones that don't break and can be easily replaced. Newspapers can be used to build furniture of most shapes and sizes. Bundles of newspapers, bound with cord and covered with large sheets of newspaper to create the desired surface, make sturdy, climbable benches, chairs, tables, and beds. They can be covered with black and white or color print. They can be painted or decorated with glossy Sunday magazine pages.

Furniture from newspaper bundles will, of course, be heavy, so if the bulky pieces have to be moved within a production, it is best to slide them on a slick surface or place them on movable platforms. Children can have fun rearranging the bundles in view of the audience and transforming a wall into benches or a bed.

▼ Newspaper Walls

1. Stack newspaper bundles tied with cord across back or sides of the set to form **walls of a fort**.

2. Stack newspaper bundles for **breakaway wall** to establish area limit for scenes.

▼ Furniture

1. Stack three or four bundles tied with cord end to end to form **bed**. You may cover them with sheets of paper for spread.

2. Stack three bundles for back of **chair** and two for chair seat.

3. Stack newspaper bundles two or three high and end to end to form a **table**.

▼ Boat

Stack newspaper bundles two or three high in shape of boat. Add a tall "T" of rolled newspaper, attach a sheet with tape or glue, and you have a mast on a pirate ship.

NEWSPAPER "WEAPONS"

Properties must be safe to use, especially in programs with younger children. Stage combat with newspaper swords, spears, knives, and guns is a much freer, more cathartic experience than with other less flexible materials. Newspapers rolled tightly with a taped-on or tied-on crosspiece become a quite acceptable sword that can't hurt anyone, even in the heat of battle. Spears and rifles—the delight of pretend soldiers—are practical, nonviolent, and easily replaced when made from newspaper.

▼ Sword

1. Roll a long length from three or four sheets of newspaper. Cut to size, or cut before rolling.

2. Tie on 6-inch crosspiece with string.

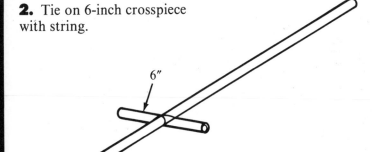

6"

▼ Spear

1. Roll spear shaft as for sword.

2. Tape or glue on a spear point cut from several thicknesses of paper.

It takes time to make realistic rifles and pistols. Before you start, weigh how much realism is needed against how much time is available. For quick exercises, a long roll will do for a rifle; for a more realistic-looking weapon, add short rolls to one end of the long roll to suggest a rifle stock. A short roll bent midway to make a handle and a barrel will do for a pirate pistol. More elaborate weapons may be extra projects carried on at home.

▼ Shotgun

For a reasonably realistic shotgun, tape or tie two 12-inch rolls to two longer rolls.

12″

▼ Pistol

For a quick pistol, bend a
12-inch roll midway.

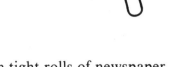

A shield can be built from tight rolls of newspaper sheets tied into a triangle and covered with a single sheet cut to fit.

▼ Shield

1. Tie rolls into a triangle and add a horizontal handle to form shield frame.

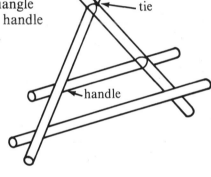

tie

handle

2. Cut a single sheet and glue or tape to shield frame.

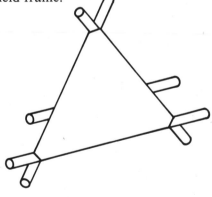

OTHER PROPS

Logs, kites, boxes, tubes, and chains can be created from newspapers. All of these are good stimulants for plot creating, story building, and mime exercises. Put a **magic wand** in a student's hand, and ask what feats of magic he or she can perform, involving the others in fantasy. Can he or she put people to sleep? Make them jump up and down? Freeze them in position?

▼ Log

Loosely roll large, full sheets and then telescope them. Cover with full sheets to create bark.

▼ Wand or Scepter

Glue a wad of paper to one end of a newspaper roll. Add whatever trim you desire.

▼ Kite

1. Make a cross-shaped frame and cover with a single sheet of newspaper cut to shape.

2. Add newspaper strips for tail.

3. For flight, stiff reeds or narrow sticks are needed.
   For decorative kites, use tightly rolled newspaper tubes in place of sticks.

4. Notch ends of cross-pieces to keep string in place.

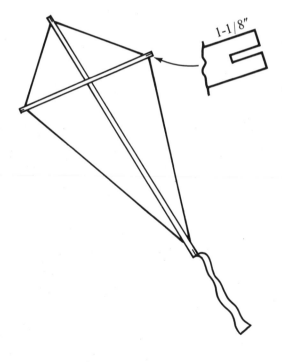

1-1/8"

Boxes can be made in many sizes to be used for treasure chests or decorations. **Paper chains** can be heavy chains or rope or decorative trim, depending on the width and length of the newspaper links (see p. 38). Fly **kites** that were used as decoration after the play's run or after a rehearsal.

▼ Box

1. Fold as shown on vertical and horizontal.

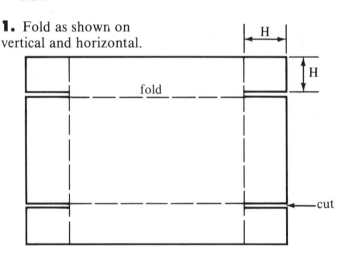

2. Box depth is determined by depth of piece when folded.

3. Cut into vertical folds as shown.

4. Place the corner of horizontal folds inside vertical folds and glue or tape.

Basic pieces for forming properties have been shown here. You can create more as the need arises. In exercises and rehearsals, the quicker the construction, the better the process. If you want more permanent newspaper properties, however, they can be painted and lacquered. Shape and more precision can come from crafting objects with papier mâché, using newspaper for the strips of layered paper. Directions for making papier mâché are in Chapter 7.

5

Making Sets and Scenery from Newspaper

The forts, castles, and ships that were created during my first experiments with Newspaper Theatre became settings for play and pretending. The carry-over to a stage happened when I began to teach. Newspaper Theatre fits well in a proscenium stage, theatre-in-the-round, or a thrust with the audience on three sides. Each can be the right place for Newspaper Theatre. Newspaper sets and scenery also give strong visual effects when captured with a video camera.

Newspaper sets and scenery can be used for fantasy plays or realistic settings. The sets and scenery can be simple and quick, such as a suggestion of furniture or a vehicle from a few bundles; or you can trim with a few sculptured pieces; or you can make an elaborate, complex creation. Use stacks of bundled newspapers to create variety in elevation. Use sheets of newspaper for texture over plain backdrop walls, or make elaborate sculptured backgrounds with newspaper. A full set made of newspaper takes time and should be a part of the time allotted for technical crafts or worked into a rehearsal or workshop program so as not to interrupt the process of creative drama. Whether simple or elaborate, however, the cost of a total set will be no more than the price of the glue, paste, string, paper clips, pins, tacks, clothespins, tape, and paint you choose to use.

Mix or match color and black and white newsprint, or use glossy Sunday magazine sheets, or use paint. Spray is quickest to apply to sculpted pieces, but you can also paint newspaper sheets before cutting and shaping. (For more on coloring newspaper, see pages 73–78).

NEWSPAPER "WALLS"

Hang newspaper from string lines when you can't tack or tape on a wall, such as those in a multipurpose room, library, or classroom. Stretch string or cord from doorjambs or freestanding posts or screens, and drop large sheets of newspaper at the fold over the cord, keeping the newspapers as close together as needed for the cover you desire. Attach sculptured pieces to the string or to the newspaper cover. Or paint or color design, texture, or pictures to form a backdrop.

PAPER SCULPTURE TRIM

Scallops, fringe, and curls are paper sculpture techniques that may be applied to costumes and properties, as well as to scenery. They make good texture for suggesting foliage and fantasy forests.

Scallops and fringe may be torn or cut with scissors. Curls come from newspaper cut into strips and then rolled tightly. For a tighter curl, dampen a curled roll and unroll it after the paper dries (this is the same principle used to curl hair). Making curls for a large area can be time-consuming, but it can be a good project with a big group when everyone has to be kept busy.

▼ Scallops

Cut or tear scallops and fringe to size.

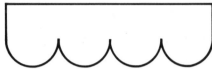

▼ Curls

Cut curls from a roll or from rolled strips cut to size. Use a paper clip or bobby pin until the curl holds.

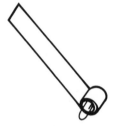

▼ Fringe

Window and door openings can be filled with long fringe or with strips cut almost to the top.

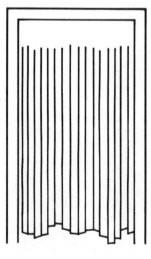

LEAVES AND FLOWERS

Flowers and leaves and vines take time, especially when covering large areas, but they can be stored and reused. There are endless variants to be discovered with experimentation. Create vines by attaching leaves and flowers to strings and ribbons; then attach them to walls or hang from ceilings, freestanding posts, and screens. The fan shapes shown in the section on properties (Chapter 4) can be used for flowers. You can also adapt patterns for tissue and crepe-paper flowers. Here are some examples to get you started.

▼ Leaf

1. Cut out leaf shapes.

2. Pinch at one end to curve.

3. Accordion-fold the other end.

4. Attach pinched end of leaf to walls, string, or ribbon to other props or to costumes.

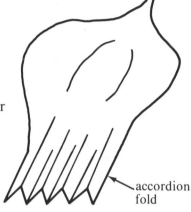

accordion fold

▼ Large Flower

1. Cut out large leaf shapes for petals.

2. Pinch and accordion-fold as for leaves.

3. Connect five or six petals at pinched ends with wire ties or tape.

4. Tape or glue small wad of paper in center of connected petals.

▼ Paper Circle Flower

1. Cut a large circle from half a sheet of newspaper. The size of the flower will depend on the size of the circle. Cut a small hole in the center of the circle.

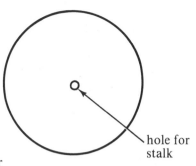

hole for stalk

2. Bunch together the inner third of the circle, like a handle with the hole at the bottom.

3. Attach to walls, strings, ribbons, or stalks made from paper rolls.

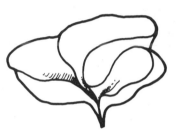

4. Paper circle flowers can be varied by cutting to separate petals or by scalloping or fringing edges.

TREES

Eucalyptus trees have numerous uses once you have mastered the simple process that was part of Orson Bean's comic routine on television back in the fifties and early sixties.

Support taller trees that won't stand upright alone by attaching them to walls, hanging them from above the set, or attaching them to posts or freestanding objects. Pot them in buckets, cans, or waste baskets for clusters of texture. Paint them before or after sculpting. The trees offer so much textural strength, however, that color is not necessary.

▼ Eucalyptus Tree

1. Overlap large sheets and roll evenly.

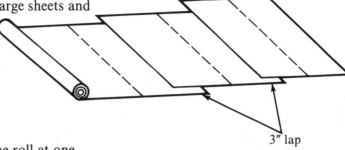

3″ lap

2. Flatten the roll at one end, and make a tear one third of the way down the roll. Flatten the end once more so the tears are at the edges, and tear down the middle again, one third of the way down the roll. You should have four equidistant tears one third of the way down the roll.

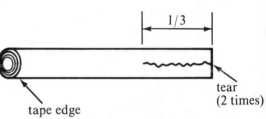

1/3

tape edge

tear (2 times)

3. Reach into center of roll at torn end and pull out inner rolls carefully, telescoping the roll.

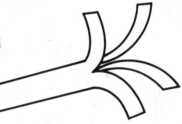

4. Shake out tree and stand it in a bucket. For a forest, attach trees to each other or to a wall.

6

Using Newspaper Text

The print on the paper can also be used in Newspaper Theatre. The material, the texture, the colors have all been considered so far in making costumes, properties, and scenery. But don't overlook the trees for the forest. The print—these countless words, the symbols of exchange and expression, the purpose of the newspaper—can be used for scripts, exercises, audition material, and just about anywhere words are needed in a creative drama program.

DICTION EXERCISES

To add variety to programs and rehearsals, take exercises for diction from newspaper articles or columns, from food and auto ads, from descriptions of photos. Older students and advanced readers can search on their own and lead less-skilled and younger readers. With groups of beginning readers or nonreaders, photos and graphics from advertisements are useful for description, discussion, and visualization recall. It's easier and cheaper to gather multiple copies of newspapers than it is to obtain textbooks. Students can bring in this week's free-to-the-house editions. Often a request at the local newspaper office will provide multiple copies of one edition. Or just pull from the newspaper piles and take turns choosing from what is available.

Consider the reading skills of the group and read aloud from editorials, or have older students read, and have the others echo the words or phrases that are good diction exercises. Select words from an article that begin with *t*'s, *d*'s, then *m*'s, and so on. With multiple copies, read together. Headlines, titles, and leaders offer lots of fun. The following two examples from the *New York Times* scan well and could be fun for all ages to repeat:

Flowers and Foliage Accent the Sturdy Kalanchoes
Of Medals, Meetings, Coins and Shows

DIALOGUE AND STORIES

Dialogue from interviews, articles, comics, or columns can be used in exercises to stimulate characterization; to practice inflection, accents, and voice modulation. Again, the older, more advanced readers can work independently, while the younger, beginning readers are guided. Beginning readers can develop dialogue based on the plethora of graphics in newspapers and photos of people and exciting events.

An exercise for beginning or nonreading youngsters could come from a picture one of them finds. Ask the children to select pictures of things that are in their homes. Have them show the pictures and show how the object is used. All could participate by making the sounds of the object, by miming the movements of the body in using the object, and by telling in a big voice what we do with the object.

This graphic advertising a telephone can be used for an exercise.

1. What sound does your telephone make?
2. Who would like to pretend they are talking on the phone?
3. What funny story about a telephone call could we imagine and pretend about?

Sketches and manuscripts can grow from selected bits of quoted speech and dialogue. A plot or setting can be built around the information given in an article or one previously used for a diction or characterization exercise. Building sketches from grocery ads can be fun. Look at the different foods. What can we have for our imaginary lunch?

This advertisement for wall paneling could be used to stimulate a sketch for all ages.

1. Where is the man?
2. Does he have a family, friends, other workers? Name them.
3. What is a problem he will have to solve? What trouble will he have as he puts up the wall?
4. Let's make a play about this man, his friends, his family, and his problem.

MOVEMENT EXERCISES

Sports pages are also good for setting off improvisational sketches, especially where the purpose is movement.

> The Jaguars' contributions to the din came in the form of bat meeting ball. Art Whiteside hit his 20th homer leading off the game, making him and shortstop Nelson Miller only the third double-play combination ever to each hit 20 homers in a season.
>
> Cliff Sanders hit two homers, one exceptional for its distance (438 feet) and another for its direction (left-center, the first of his 26 homers to go to the opposite field).
>
> These three blasts led the Jaguars' to a 6–3 victory over Union City, a triumph that produced a crash that many people never would have believed could happen, especially within earshot of Bill Taylor.

1. Select volunteers to reenact the parts of the key figures, showing the activity in slow motion.
2. Have the rest of the group mimic each movement once it is satisfactory.
3. Use the activity to develop mime sketches.
4. Let the activity reported in the newspaper be broadened to slapstick comedy.

Quarterback Henry Herndon threw for one touchdown and set up two more as fourth-ranked Jersey State defeated Winyard, 31–6, in a sloppily played game on a wet field.

Herndon, who played three quarters, completed 13 of 20 passes for 156 yards and ran for 38 more on six carries for the Jersey Jaguars (4–0). The White Knights fell to 3–1–1.

The officials marked off 16 penalties for 186 yards as the players sloshed and slipped on the wet turf. Jersey State was assessed 103 yards on nine penalties and Winyard 83 on seven.

"We took foolish penalties and showed a lack of poise," Jersey State coach Tom Gregorio said. "This club was aggressive, which you want, and physically tough. . . . You can't be aggressive and not have penalties, but some of ours are nonsense, just plain old-fashioned nonsense."

Audition materials from newspapers can substitute for the playbooks that arrive late or when there aren't enough copies of the play for all who should read. Again, it is easy to obtain multiple copies. Older children who are good readers can have fun when two or more read aloud from different articles, attempting to convey rational meaning to a back-and-forth exchange. Each reads a sentence, and the purpose is to suggest a rational conversation, regardless of the absurdity of the exchange. This not only makes for a good loosening-up exercise, but can also show how open and free older students are in audition.

Beginning readers can use special school publications with graded vocabulary or newspaper supplements from the special educational service programs of large dailies. All ages can use photos and graphics. If the purpose of the audition is to hear the voice and see how the child moves, the group leader—adult or student—can ask each child to find a picture and tell about it. The only limit is the imagination of the leader and the children.

Newspaper text is so plentiful, so readily available, so appropriate for varied use and experimentation that this kind of recycling is a pleasure.

7

Newspaper Plus . . .

The Newspaper Theatre payoff is unique: you can have a drama program with newspapers as construction material and newspaper text as inspiration. Newspaper can be supplemented, however, with other free or inexpensive materials.

COLORING NEWSPAPER

In addition to the colors in Sunday comics, magazines, and the color print some large newspaper publishers are now using, color can be added in several ways. You can brush on poster paint or thick water colors, or use marking pens or crayons or spray paint. The aerosol cans are comparatively cheap and cover fast. Spray paint makes a good preservative for hats, masks, costumes, and props.

Use spray paints cautiously. They should be used in a well-ventilated room or, even better, out of doors. If the students are young, adults should do the spraying; older students should be closely supervised. Appropriate clothing and hand covers are necessary to protect against paint splatter. Be conservative because paint is the most expensive item in your Newspaper Theatre budget.

PAPIER MÂCHÉ

Papier mâché has many uses in Newspaper Theatre. Because it provides structure, it is good for more permanent props and scenery. Finished, well-crafted papier mâché takes time and skill, so be sure of your needs before deciding to use it.

For rough, temporary, quick pieces, use white flour or wheat paste (which can be purchased in hardware stores and provides a smoother and better medium), water, and strips of newspaper layered over molds.

Make a flour-paste mixture by placing half a cup of flour or wheat paste in a throwaway container. Add water slowly, beginning with a quarter of a cup, until the paste is smooth and fluid, not solid.

The size of the strips or pieces of newspaper you use for the layers in the papier mâché depends on the surface angles. If you are simply covering a large flat area, such as a shield, use big pieces. Place a layer of paper, add a covering of paste, add another sheet of paper, and so on.

For a smaller object or an object with more planes, angles, or curves, such as a ball or box, use small strips, building the shape as you lay on the paste and the paper. Avoid too much water, and be sure you allow time for drying (usually at least overnight).

TRASH BAGS AND VINYL SHEETS

Plastic trash bags give color and texture variety, and they can be obtained easily. Students can each bring one or two from home. Explore supermarkets and hardware stores to see where the most colorful can be obtained.

Vinyl sheets can be obtained in large quantity from paint stores, hardware stores, and most home-improvement centers. They can cost almost as much as paint, but the quantity goes a long way. Combining vinyl sheets with trash bags gives more color choice and the extra fun of transparency from the clear bags. Mix colors for added interest.

Mixed with newspaper foliage, flat **leaf shapes** cut from trash bags or from sheets of vinyl give a fantasy forest another dimension. Enough flat surfaces to reflect light will suggest an equatorial forest; a wet look. Space-fantasy settings with plastic trash bags take on a futuristic high-tech look because the material is so contemporary.

If you need **elevations or rocky protuberances**, cover bundles of newspaper with vinyl or trash bags.

Decorative or functional **rocks and boulders** can be made quickly by stuffing trash bags with newspaper wads and connecting some at the neck with ties or string. When the boulders stack, they stay together. If a rockslide occurs, they all go together.

Cover backdrops or back-wall areas with **abstract designs** cut from vinyl, trash bags, and newspaper. Patterns cut from the flat sheets of material can be overlapped. To connect the vinyl or trash bags, you'll need to use pins, tacks, or tape. If you're not allowed to pin, tack, or tape on the back wall, overlay it with newspaper as suggested in Chapter 5, then attach the plastic pieces to the newspaper with pins, staples, or paper clips.

Trash bags and newspaper can be used in combination for **varied costume effects**. Plastic holds up longer and drapes more easily than newspaper. A small plastic rectangle might be added to the Foreign Legion hat for the back drape, or become an apron over a newspaper tunic, or a cape attached to a tunic and tied separately. Again, the plastic must be connected with ties, tape, or fasteners. Glue or paste won't work.

ALUMINUM FOIL

Foil also adds variety to newspaper backdrops and sets. It is expensive in quantity, but a few purchased rolls used sparingly will not inflate budgets too badly. Sometimes, students can bring a roll from home to donate to the production.

Foil is a great **high-tech addition** to space fantasies or for machines and technological environments. A **rain curtain** made by hanging foil strips from a wire is cheaper than purchasing or renting a ready-made rain curtain. If you have a large area to cover, alternate foil strips with vinyl and newspaper strips.

▼ Rain Curtain

1. Cut the strips to allow some folding over at the top.

2. Tape or use paper clips to secure top of strips to wire or wood.

3. For a door-length rain curtain, glue, paste, or tape newspaper strips together. Vinyl and aluminum foil can be cut in the necessary lengths.

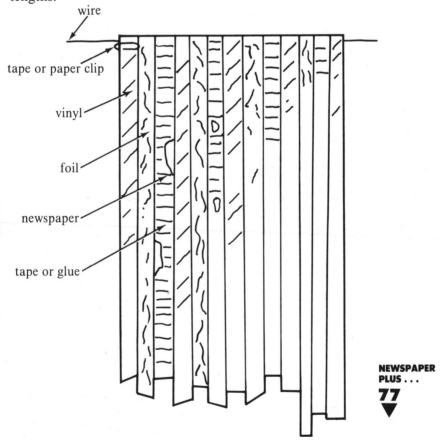

wire

tape or paper clip

vinyl

foil

newspaper

tape or glue

CLOTH AND CARDBOARD

Cloth and cardboard are good mixes with newspaper for backdrop variety, and they can be gathered without cost. Where drape effects are needed, use scrap fabrics or worn sheets, bedspreads, drapes, or tablecloths.

Alien and exotic terrain are easily built from pasting fabric and newspaper together, especially to cover odd-shaped three-dimensional objects, such as cave openings or ship hulls. Cardboard boxes and sheets of cardboard are good stiffeners—and they have enough potential on their own to justify a manual for Cardboard Theatre.

The rules for Newspaper Theatre can be revised, broken, and renewed at will. The joy is having an endless supply of free material that is rich with history, culture, and universal significance. When you begin to work with Newspaper Theatre, you will wonder how you could ever have overlooked its potential.

When you have funds for costumes and sets and materials, use them and live in luxury. When you don't, continue to develop your program, your performers, your goals for creative expression and exchange in the drama program—and, above all, don't despair: you can always do Newspaper Theatre.